christmas

christmas

20 CAN-DO PROJECTS

Karin Hossack

MQP

Published by MQ Publications Limited
12 The Ivories, 6–8 Northampton Street,
London N1 2HY
Tel: 020 7359 2244
Fax: 020 7359 1616
email: mail@mqpublications.com
www.mqpublications.com
Copyright © MQ Publications Limited 2004

Designer: Mark Latter
Thank you for their work on the projects to Deborah Schneebeli Morrell (p.12, p.60, p.72) and Dorothy Wood (P.64).

ISBN: 1 84072 829 9

1 3 5 7 9 0 8 6 4 2

Printed and bound in China

contents

introduction

For many of us, Christmas is a special time of year, a time of celebration and goodwill. It is given to entertaining, when family and friends draw close. For children it is magical, filled with the promise of a visit from Santa and a stocking full of exciting gifts. Christmas is also the time of year when we lavish attention on our homes. We spend more time on our homes at Christmas that at any other time of year, filling it full of festive cheer with twinkling lights and colorful ornaments. Good-quality Christmas decorations can be expensive, and it is perhaps more personal to make them yourself—the whole family can get involved with these projects that take a fresh look at traditional Christmas decor.

Christmas is for those of us who enjoy the festive preparations, who relish the challenge of decorating our homes and making projects, and without it costing a fortune or taking too much time and effort. This little book offers a warm and comfortable choice that is elegant, appealing, and thoroughly modern. The overall scheme is fresh and unfussy, with pine greenery in abundance and a wealth of projects that are understated in their elegance. Whether your home is an urban flat or a rural cottage, each project can be adapted to suit the environment in which it will be displayed and to suit your personal style and color scheme.

This book features a range of tasteful and innovative yuletide decorations for you to make. The choice of projects is

deliberately restrained, no glitzy baubles or tired old tinsel—these were consigned to the attic. Instead there is a range of projects which make effective use of materials that can be found around the home or in the garden. While many are traditional, such as the Felt Tree Skirt and Christmas Stocking, there are also unusual novelties that are appropriately seasonal. The Ribbon and Ornament Curtain, for instance, decorates a corner that might not otherwise receive any decorative treatment at all and it can be enjoyed as much from the outside of the house as from within.

Several projects are inspired by different eras of history and by the traditions of cultures throughout the world. The Cut-Paper Shelf Edging, for example, is inspired by the intricate paper-cutting techniques of Mexico, the narrative paper-cut window decoration is inspired by Swiss folk art, and the Christmas Wheat Sheaf is an idea adapted from rural Scandinavia.

These projects are all suitable for beginners willing to try their hand at a new skill and no project requires a trip

to a specialist store for unheard of or fanciful materials. They do not require massive amounts of preparation, assembly time, or well-honed craft skills. Whatever your level of ability, or however much time you are left with to prepare for the event, *Christmas* is sure to inspire your decorating ideas, gifts, and home accessories.

decorative
bird
greeting card

These beautiful embossed metal Christmas cards are so simple
to make and decorate using a tracing wheel and punched stars.
They are an ideal gift that would look stunning on anyone's
mantelpiece. The enduring quality of the warm-colored copper
metal also means that the motif can be removed from the card
and re-used for another decorative purpose after the festive season.

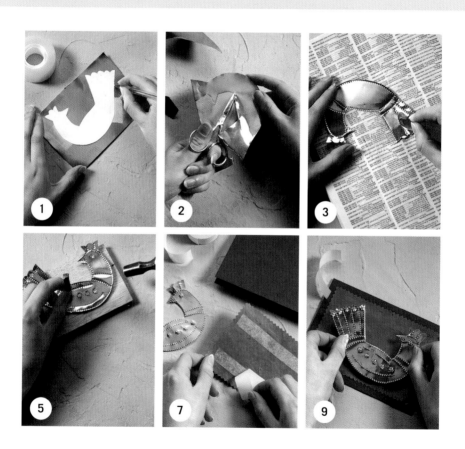

0.004in/0.1mm-thick
copper foil

Tracing paper and pencil

Thin card stock and glue

Transparent tape

Double-sided tape

Old phone book

Dry ballpoint pen

Brown card stock—
6¼ x 8½in/16 x 22cm

Tracing wheel

Blue handmade paper
6¼ x 3½in/16 x 9cm

Small-pointed scissors

Pinking shears

Star punch and hammer

Small piece of wood

1 To make a template, trace or photocopy the pattern provided (p.88). Stick the copy to card and cut out. Tape the template to the copper. Draw the outline with a ballpoint pen pressing lightly to transfer the design.

2 Remove the template. Cut out the shape.

3 Place the shape right side down on an old phone book. Outline the shape, pressing firmly with the tracing wheel. "Draw" two parallel lines at the base of the neck, then four lines to separate the tail from the body.

4 With the tracing wheel, draw two lines at each side of the wing.

5 Transfer the bird to the wood surface. Using a hammer, punch one star for the eye, five along the center of the wing, and five along the tip of the tail.

6 Fold the brown card stock in half so that it stands with the opening at the base.

7 Trim the edge of the blue paper with pinking shears. Apply two strips of double-sided tape to one side.

8 Center the blue rectangle, then stick in place on the brown card stock.

9 Center the bird on the paper and stick in place using the double-sided tape.

10 Press lightly to ensure the bird is secure.

folded paper
pine cones

The simple yet intricate pattern of these folded patchwork-style pine cones is really striking. They make wonderful alternative Christmas tree decorations and have a simple, contemporary look. These ornaments are easy to make using a variety of pretty handmade papers, polystyrene eggs, craft pins, and threads.

A selection of 3in/7.5cm
polystyrene eggs

Light-weight handmade papers
in a variety of colors—two
colors (A and B) per egg

Sequin and bead craft pins

Metallic glass bead-head
craft pins

Lamé embroidery thread

Straight edge or ruler

Paper scissors

1 On each of two sheets of contrasting color paper, measure and mark 1¾in/ 4.5cm wide strips down the length of each sheet. Carefully cut each strip.

2 To make the folded triangle, on one strip, fold the corner of a short end in towards the long side so that straight edges are aligned. Cut the excess strip away from the folded triangle. Make 26 from color A and 24 from color B.

3 Fold each triangle in half. Cut one 1in/2.5cm square of color A. Cover the narrow end of the egg with the square and mold to fit. Pin the corners.

4 Place four triangles of color B over the paper square so that the triangle tips meet at the tip of the egg. Pin each triangle in place on the two narrow points using craft pins. Insert the pins at an angle.

5 Position four triangles of color A ¼in/0.75cm below row 1 and pin in place, so that the tip is staggered between the tops of the previous row.

6 Continue to alternate the colored rows, working around the form and keeping the triangles evenly spaced so that no gaps or pin heads are visible.

7 When you reach the end, carefully overlap the last four triangles. Cover all of the cut edges with a small square cut from the same color paper. Pin temporarily into place.

8 Make a lamé thread bow. Place on the end of the egg and pin through all the layers with a craft pin.

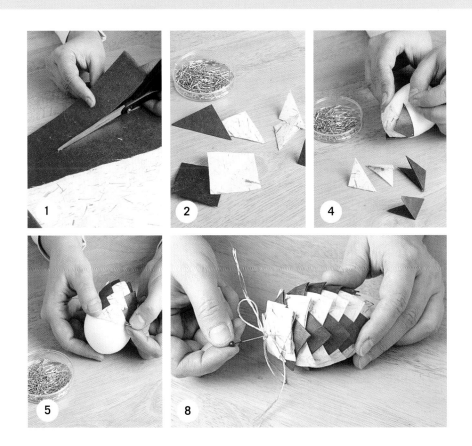

ribbon and ornament curtain

This innovative ribbon curtain adds a sparkle of Christmas color to an otherwise dull corner and adds cheer to an undecorated window. It presents the perfect opportunity to use up all those ornaments that will not fit on the tree and requires minimal sewing skills. The effect is simple, uncluttered, and elegant.

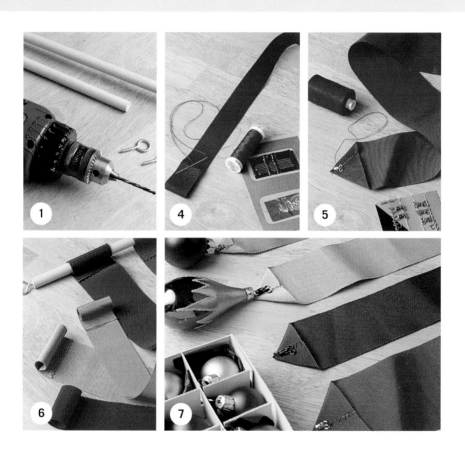

½ in/1.5cm diameter dowel to fit the width of the window

Two screw eyes

Two screw hooks

A variety of widths of grosgrain ribbon in assorted colors

Sewing thread to match ribbon colors

Sewing kit

Dressmaker's hook and eyes— one for each ribbon used

Saw and drill

Assorted Christmas ornaments —one for each ribbon

Paint to match shade of ribbons

Paint brush

1 Measure the length and width of your window. Cut the dowel to fit the width of the window frame. Drill holes into the ends of the dowel and screw in the eyelets. Measure and mark the dowel position on the window frame. Drill holes in alignment with the screw eyes and screw the hooks in place. Paint the ends of the dowel to match the main color of the ribbons, then let dry.

2 Arrange the ribbon lengths side by side on a flat surface. To gauge the length of this ribbon, measure the height of the window, then deduct 12in/30cm. The shortest ribbons are half the length of the middle ribbon. The remaining ribbons taper from the middle to the sides.

3 Add 2in/5cm to each length for seams. Drape the ribbons over the dowel and pin in place to check the fit

at the window. Stick small pieces of masking tape to the top of each ribbon, numbering them in order.

4 Make a 2in/5cm loop in the top of a piece of ribbon and, using a matching thread color, sew it down. Make sure that the fold is straight, if it is crooked the ribbon will hang incorrectly. Sew all the ribbons in the same way.

5 To make the bottom edges, fold both corners to the back, to form a point. Sew the turned in edges, working from the point to the upper edge. Sew a dressmaker's hook close to the tip of each ribbon at the back.

6 Slide all ribbons onto the dowel in the correct order.

7 Attach a selection of ornaments onto the hooks at the back of the ribbon to complete the effect.

magical
foil reindeer

It takes minimal skill, tools, and techniques to make this magical herd of reindeer, which will look charming on a Christmas mantelpiece or arranged under a simply-decorated tree. To make a wintry set for the animals, make a backdrop of forest trees from some slightly thicker aluminum foil. Alternatively, you can make them into a mobile by carefully threading them onto a wire frame.

0.004in/0.1mm-thick
aluminum foil—
6in/15cm square for
each reindeer
Tracing paper and pencil
Thin card stock and glue
Dry ballpoint pen
Transparent tape
Small-pointed scissors
Old phone book
Bent-nose pliers

1 To make a template, trace or photocopy the pattern provided (p.93). Stick the copy to card stock and cut out.

2 Tape the templates onto the aluminum foil. Draw around each outline.

3 Remove the templates. Carefully cut out each shape using small-pointed scissors. Take special care with the antlers.

4 Place the shapes on an old phone book. Mark the body pattern by pressing with a dry ballpoint pen. Mark short lines along the back and then at right angles down the legs. Mark the eye, mouth, antlers, and neck.

5 Cut a ⅛in/0.5cm slit at each side of the base of the neck, ⅛in/0.5cm up from the base. Turn the cut sections in and press flat.

6 Make a slit in the front of the reindeer body large enough to fit the base of the neck through. Push the neck through the slit.

7 To secure the head firmly to the body, turn the reindeer's body to the wrong side and use the pliers to open out the folded-in sections. Bend the tab at the front of the body down, then bend the body over to enable the reindeer to stand.

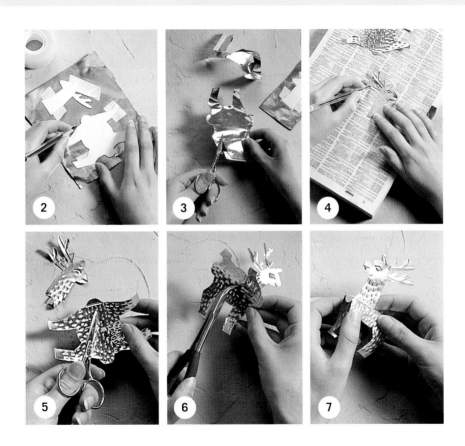

christmas stocking

As a symbol of bounty and giving, a stocking hanging by the hearth adds the finishing touch to your Christmas decorations. The instructions are for the red stocking pictured, but they can be personalized with any number of decorative features, including hand-embroidered snowflakes, punched holes, and felt leaves.

MATERIALS

20 x 36in/50 x 100cm main color felt for stocking

20 x 8in/50 x 20cm contrast color felt for cuff

12in/30cm square contrast color felt for the decoration

Sewing kit

Craft glue

Scissors

Templates

Hand and machine embroidery thread to match all three colors of felt

1 Enlarge the patterns provided (p.90) on a photocopier to measure 17½in/44.5cm from the top to the bottom of the heel.

2 Cut out the photocopies. Draw around the stocking and the cuff on the correct color of felt. Cut two of each.

3 From scraps of felt cuff, cut a strip ⅓ x 8in/1 x 20cm. Use this to make a strong hanging loop.

4 Embroider the six-point stars in a random pattern on the front and back of the stocking if using, with three strands of hand embroidery thread.

5 With right sides together stitch the top of each cuff to the top of each stocking. Sew the cuff side seams together pressing the seam allowance in the same direction on both sides.

6 Stitch the two halves of the stocking together using a ¼in/0.75cm seam. Fold the cuff down. Embroider a six-pointed star on the cuff. Cut out the decoration in the contrasting color and stick onto the cuff with craft glue.

7 Fold the hanging loop in half lengthwise. Sew through both layers, from end to end using matching thread. Fold the loop in half and baste the two ends together. Sew in place inside back of cuff.

cut-paper shelf edging

This sophisticated shelf edging is made using techniques similar to the way children cut shapes out of folded paper to make snowflakes or paper chains. The traditional paper-cutting skills of Mexican craftsmen have been adapted to make this decoration and the simple design is intended to be cut six layers at a time using a craft knife and cutting mat.

Roll of colored waxed paper

Roll of white or transparent
waxed paper

Cutting mat

Craft knife

Paper clips and black marker

Pinking shears

1 Measure the width of your shelf and determine the drop of the edging. Enlarge the template (p.91) to fit an even number of times into the shelf width. Define the shapes with a black marker. For a long shelf, make several copies.

2 Cut the required length of colored and white waxed paper where necessary, sticking together. Fold each length accordion-style to the same width as the template.

3 Slide the template into the folded colored paper between the third and fourth fold. Make sure that you can see the definition of the design lines through the top layer. If there are more than six layers, unfold the extra layers from the bottom of the stack and leave them to one side.

4 Secure all four corners of the stack with paper clips to prevent the folds from slipping.

5 Place the stack on the cutting mat and carefully cut out the design. With a new blade you should be able to cut through six layers of paper and the template at the same time. Use a new template for each stack of six sheets.

6 Cut the scalloped edge with pinking shears. Remove the paper clips. Slide a template inside the white waxed paper as before. Draw the scalloped edge with a pencil. Remove the template and cut on the line using pinking shears.

7 Unfold both accordions. Place the white paper behind the colored paper, all edges aligned. Slide the white paper down so that it sits 1in/2.5cm below the colored paper. Stick the layers together. Fold the top edge over so that it creates a shelf lining, or cut it off and stick both layers to the edge of the shelf.

angel
tree lights

Disguise your usual Christmas lights with this innovative angel design made from non-flammable white polypropylene plastic. Don't let the unusual material stop you from making these novel lights—it is readily available from good craft suppliers. The angels are so easy to make by drawing around the simple template provided and cutting out the shapes using pinking shears.

A sheet of white
polypropylene plastic

Template plastic or
medium-weight cardboard

Scissors

Pencil

Paper hole punch

Pinking shears

½in/1cm leather hole punch

Small piece of plywood

Hammer

String of standard tree lights

1 To make a template, photocopy the pattern provided (p.92). Glue the copy to cardboard and cut out. Punch the holes marked on the pattern using a paper hole punch.

2 Onto white polypropylene plastic draw around the template. Mark the holes and cutting lines.

3 Cut around each shape using pinking shears. Cut the head and arms with scissors.

4 With the piece of plywood for a surface, use the leather punch and a hammer to punch the marked holes.

5 Carefully wrap the wings around so that they overlap and slot together.

6 Align the holes in the wings and stick onto the tree lights so that they grip the rubber base of the light fittings.

beaded
flower holder

The beadwork on these flower holders looks delicate and intricate, but the work involved is minimal. Once the beaded strands are wired together, these beautiful containers are very sturdy. They are sure to be admired as a very special gift and can either be wrapped around a small pot of seasonal flowers or filled with a small gift wrapped in colorful tissue paper.

MATERIALS

⅛in/4mm seed beads in two colors (A and B)

¼in/6mm pressed glass beads —14 for each pot (C)

Round-nose pliers

Flat-nose pliers

Wire snippers

0.025in/0.6mm silver-plated wire

Glass container to insert in holder

Fresh flowers

Foliage

Florist's oasis block

1 For each beaded pot, cut one length of wire 7in/18cm long. With round nose pliers, form a ⅛in/2mm closed loop in one end. This is the base wire for the holder. Cut 14 lengths of wire 3½in/9cm long. Form a ⅛in/2mm closed loop in one end of each, these are the eye pins.

2 Thread four seed beads (B) on the base wire. Thread on an eye pin, then four more beads and an eye pin, and so on. Thread on 56 beads in total finishing with an eye pin.

4 Pick up the open end of the wire in the round-nose pliers. Thread on the loop at the opposite end and the loop of the last eye pin. Twist the wire to close the loop.

5 Arrange the beadwork on a flat work surface. Stand one eye pin up and thread the following beads on: 1xB, 1xA, 1xB, 2xA, 1xB, 3xA,

1xB, 4xA, 1xB, 3xA, 1xB, 2xA, 1xB, 1xA. Repeat on each eye pin—322 beads in all. Form a ⅛in/2mm loop in the top of each eye pin.

6 For the top band of the pot, cut a 14in/35cm length of wire. Form a ⅛in/2mm loop in one end. Thread the wire through a loop at the top of an eye pin.

7 Onto the top band of wire, thread on the following beads: 2xA, 1xC, 2xA, then slide on the next eye pin. Repeat until each eye pin is threaded onto the top band and the beading pattern is even. Trim the top band wire leaving 1½in/3.75cm excess. Make a loop in the end and hook the loop onto the first loop to form a circle.

8 To make the scalloped edge, cut seven lengths of wire 3¼in/8cm long. Form a small loop at one end of each wire. On each, thread the following seed beads: 4xA, 1xB, 1xA, 1xB, 4xA. Form an open loop at the free end. Bend each wire into a crescent.

9 Loop one open end of a crescent wire onto the top band next to a bead C. Use flat-nosed pliers to bend the loop closed. Pick up the opposite end with pliers and attach it to the wire between the 9th and 10th beads.

10 Close the loop onto the wire. Continue around the top beaded band.

11 Bend the whole form with your fingers, pushing the wire ribbing to form around a small pot or glass bowl. Fill with fresh cut flowers or a small topiary herb plant.

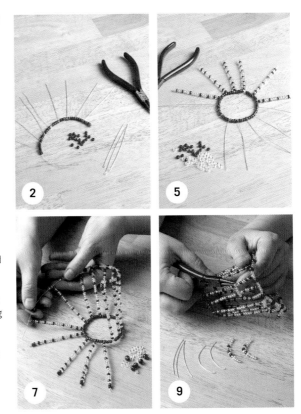

frosted
window
stencils

Frosted windows are an easy way to add festive charm to your home and your handiwork can be appreciated from both sides of the glazing. Making accurate stencils for the traditional prancing deer, decorative foliage, and folk art floral motifs takes practice, but the effect is worth the effort. To create the repeat pattern, the motifs are simply flipped to create mirror images.

MATERIALS

Glass etch spray can
Spray mount
Craft knife
Cutting mat
Newspaper

1 Photocopy or trace the three designs provided (p.94–96), enlarging each to fit your window. You will need four copies each of the flower and leaf designs and eight copies of the reindeer.

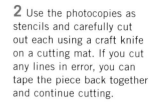

2 Use the photocopies as stencils and carefully cut out each using a craft knife on a cutting mat. If you cut any lines in error, you can tape the piece back together and continue cutting.

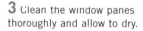

3 Clean the window panes thoroughly and allow to dry.

4 Place the stencils right side down on a sheet of newspaper. Spray lightly with spray mount and apply all the stencils in the desired order to the window panes.

5 Apply glass etch spray over the window surface, following the manufacturer's instructions. A soft even coat applied twice works best.

6 Allow to dry, then peel away the stencils.

7 To remove the etch spray, scrape away with a single-edged razor or blade.

felt
tree skirt

Wrap unsightly metal stands or practical containers with this felt tree skirt, which has been designed with warmth and simplicity in mind and with simple seasonal motifs that do not detract attention from the tree. Felt is an easy fabric to work with, and the motifs chosen mean that no sewing skills are required. The holly leaves, stems and berries are simply glued in place with fabric adhesive.

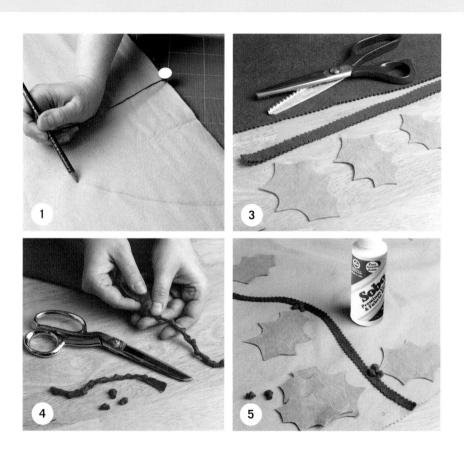

MATERIALS

1¼yd/1.2m square of felt in main color

½yd/0.5m each of contrasting colors for holly leaves and stems

¾in/2cm-wide strips of red felt for berries

Craft glue

Thumb tack

Scissors and tape measure

Pinking shears

Tracing paper and pencil

Medium-weight cardboard

Length of string or twine

1 To make the felt circle, fold the main color in half. Find the center of the folded edge and mark this point with a thumb tack. Tie one end of the string around the pin. Measure 25½in/65cm along the length of string and cut. Tie the free end to a pencil. Working on a flat surface, hold the pin in place and at the same time hold the pencil so that the string stays taut and even. Draw an arc from one folded edge around to the other side. Measure 4in/10cm from the pin and in the same way draw a small circle. Cut out both circles using pinking shears.

2 Using scissors, cut across one side of the folded edge, from the center, so that the skirt can be opened.

3 From the patterns provided (p.91) make templates for the holly leaves. Trace the shapes. Stick the tracing

paper on cardboard and cut out. On your choice of felt color, draw around each template. Cut nine small, nine medium and 18 large leaves. For the stems, cut ¾in/2cm wide strips each 23¾in/60cm long using pinking shears.

4 For the berries, cut six strips of felt ¼ x 23¾in/ 0.75 x 60cm. Tie each length into a chain of knots. Cut each knot from the chain to make 81 knots.

5 Open out the tree skirt. Arrange the stems 31in/80cm apart at the outside edge. Bend each stem into a wavy line and lightly glue the stems in place. On each stem place one small, medium, and large holly leaf. Begin with the smallest leaves at the center of the skirt. Lightly glue each leaf in place. Glue 1 to 3 berries at the top of each leaf.

twig
reindeer

These serene and elegant reindeer are quickly constructed from
the branches of a dogwood bush and they make a charming table
centerpiece. The skills required to make these exquisite decorations
are simple—a whole herd will have appeared before you know it!
No two will ever be alike and the challenge, and the fun, is in
manipulating the branches into the correct shape.

Selection of dry dogwood
branches and twigs

Prunning shears

Hot glue gun and glue

Natural color twine

Embroidery needle

1 Cut four pieces of a medium-thick branch 3in/8cm long for each body.

2 For a front leg and the head cut a branched twig 9in/24cm long and 1½in/4cm long where it branches off for the head.

3 For the second front leg, cut one twig 5½in/14cm long matching the thickness to the first leg. Cut this twig at a sharp angle at the top.

4 From a forked branch, cut the antlers 5in/12cm long, with a ½in/1cm stem.

5 Cut the back legs in the same way, ensuring the height matches the front legs, and the form will stand evenly.

6 Using the glue gun, stick together the twigs to form the reindeer's body. Firmly press the twigs together to form a flat panel.

7 Glue on the head/front leg, attaching it to the front side of the body. Add the second front leg to the other side of the body.

8 Adhere the stem at the top of the back legs to the rear of the body. Then glue the reindeer antlers to the back of the head.

9 Thread an embroidery needle with a length of natural colored twine and wrap the thread around the point where the head and antlers join. Tie the ends to secure, then trim the ends close to the twigs.

10 In the same way wrap twine around the leg and body joints on the front and back of the deer.

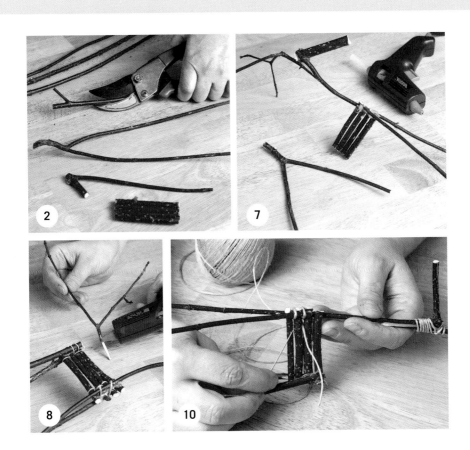

pierced paper doves

Recreate a timeless classic decoration for your tree with these unusual, but extremely elegant, pierced paper doves, which were inspired by the Victorian era. They look intricate, but are deceptively easy to make and once you begin, you may find yourself creating a whole flock in no time!

Two or three sheets of
decorated or textured
handmade paper

Choice of colors of metallic
finish giftwrap paper

Lamé embroidery thread

Scissors, pencil, and ruler

Folded towel or blanket

Glue stick

Medium-weight craft cardboard
for templates

Large embroidery needle

1 To make the templates, enlarge the patterns provided (p.92) to the desired size. Then stick the copy onto cardboard and cut out.

2 On the wrong side of the decorated paper, draw around the body A, wing span B, and wing details D templates. Use the metallic paper for the scalloped wing edges C and for the tail E.

3 Cut two of each shape except for the wing span which only requires one.

4 Place the dove pieces right side down on a folded towel. Using the embroidery needle and following the pattern on the templates, punch holes through the paper. This step can be worked using two or three pieces of paper together at a time.

5 Glue the curved edge only of wing D to the wing span B. Glue the scalloped wing C to the underside of the wing span B. When dry use your finger to curl out the scalloped edges on the glued pieces.

6 Glue each metallic tail E to a decorated paper tail E. Glue each dove tail to the underside of each body. Right sides together, fold the wing span B in half across the tab. Glue half of the tab to the underside of the body, just behind the neck bend.

7 Glue on the other side of the body. Bend the wing span B into position.

8 Using a 8in/20cm length of lamé thread, make a stitch through the edge of the body where the wings have been glued. Make a loop and tie with a knot.

embossed
velvet
tablecloth

Sumptuous velvet in a rich, jewel-like shade is perfect for an elegant Christmas dining table. The innovative and remarkably simple technique of embossing the velvet using rubber stamps with seasonal motifs makes a truly stunning tablecloth—and it can even be washed in the machine without fear of ruining the pile.

MATERIALS

Rayon or polyester velvet—
1¼yd/1.2m square, or
dimensions to suit your table

Selection of large rubber
stamps 4–5in/10–12cm

Iron

Workbench

Sewing thread to match
the velvet

Sewing kit

1 Select two or three large rubber stamps in festive and complementary designs.

2 Decide on the approximate position of each stamp—make a sketch, or mark the back of the velvet with a piece of chalk. Keep the pattern random, alternating the motifs and placing them at different angles.

3 Choose one stamp and clamp it to your workbench. This will stop the stamp from moving which can cause double images.

4 Place the velvet over the rubber stamp, nap side down, where you want the image to appear.

5 Take a hot, dry iron and firmly press down onto the back of the velvet over the rubber stamp. Hold for five seconds. Use the heel of the iron and avoid the steam holes as these will leave an impression on the velvet.

6 Repeat this process with all the rubber stamps to complete your design.

7 To finish the tablecloth, roll in the edges of the velvet to the wrong side and blindhem stitch in place using the matching sewing thread.

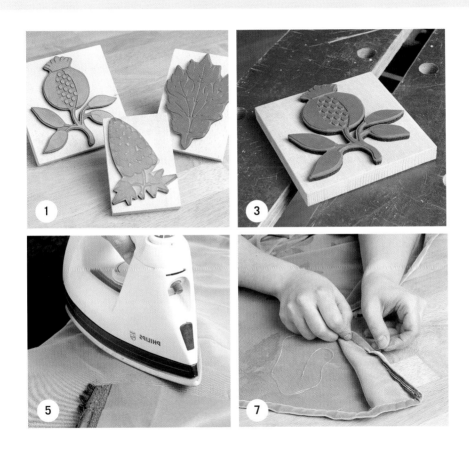

wire
tree
decorations

These simple candy-striped decorations incorporate wirework skills on a small scale. Create the candy stripe by twisting in a strand of pink aluminum wire—discarded telephone or electrical wire are colorful alternatives. The wire is bent into scrolls to form elegant pendant shapes and the beads can be chosen to complement your other Christmas tree ornaments.

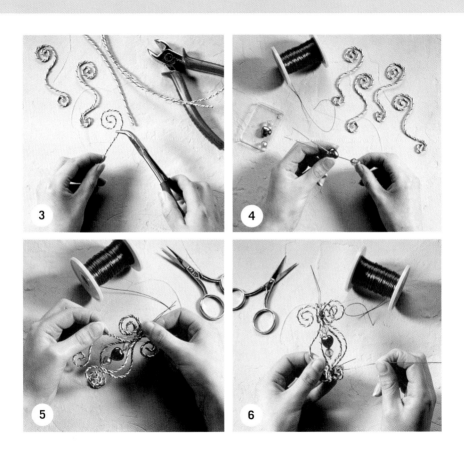

MATERIALS

0.05in/1.25mm-thick
(18 gauge) galvanized
wire—one roll

0.02in/0.5mm-thick (26 gauge)
pink anodized aluminum wire—
a small reel

Wire cutters

Bent-nose pliers

Glass beads—two small
opaque, one red heart, two
pink cut-glass

Small scissors

1 Twist together the finer wire first by wrapping the wire in two around a fixed point such as a stair banister. Feed the two cut ends into the chuck of a hand drill or wrap them around a wooden spoon. Keep the wire taut and twist the wire to the required tension.

2 Bend the thicker wire around the same fixed point and twist all the thicknesses of wire together.

3 Using wire cutters, cut four lengths of twisted wire each 8¾in/22cm. Form one end of each length into a large loose spiral. Make a curve in the central section, then form a tight spiral at the other end. Make four.

4 Cut one length of pink wire 8¾in/22cm. Thread an opaque bead half way along. Bend the wire in two around the bead, then thread the remaining beads onto both wires.

5 Put the four scrolls together, with the bend facing outwards. Place the beaded wire in the center of the large scroll. Tightly bind the top join approximately eight times with pink wire, adding a hanging loop at the top.

6 Twist the ends together to secure, then bind the base in the same manner. Open out the shape, ensuring that the scrolls are evenly spaced.

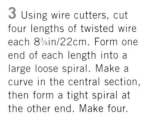

pomegranate
pyramid

Painted gold, this exquisite pomegranate pyramid is built around a florist's oasis foundation and makes for a dramatic Christmas dinner centerpiece. Use a selection of different-sized dried pomegranates so that they decrease in size from the bottom of the pyramid to the top and look out for other dried fruits and plants in various sizes and in complementary colors.

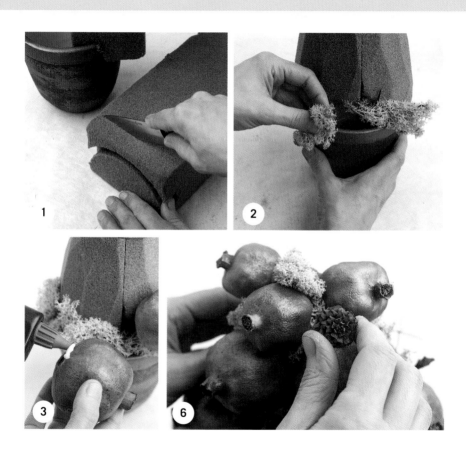

MATERIALS

1 Hold two blocks of the oasis over the plant pot and push down hard to form an impression. Cut to shape, then fit into the pot. Cut the oasis which stands above the rim of the pot at an angle to form a 1¾–2in/4–5cm circle at the top. Begin to slice down to form a cone shape.

2 Wrap a piece of florists' wire around the oasis to hold the top together. Cut more florists' wire into 2in/5cm lengths and bend in half. Break the moss up into walnut-size pieces, discarding the dark ends. Cover the oasis above the edge of the pot with moss securing each piece with a wire loop.

3 Rub the top half of each pomegranate with gold metallic paste. Use the glue gun to apply a circle of glue around the base of one of the largest pomegranates. Press the fruit into the oasis quite firmly to

make a dent and hold for a few moments as the glue sets.

4 Grade the pomegranates so that the largest will be at the base of the cone. Stick each to the oasis in an irregular pattern with wide gaps between each. Continue adding moss and pomegranates until the surface is covered.

5 Fill in the larger spaces with dried flowerheads. Use red and cream plant material which blends in with the pomegranates. Break the heads off with a length of stalk which can be pushed directly into the oasis.

6 Use the litchi nuts to fill in the last small spaces. These can be wired by drilling two small holes in the base or stuck in place with a glue gun.

7 Apply a small amount of gold paint to all the dried plant material to finish.

herald angels swag

Let these exquisite angels proclaim Christmas for you with a joyful song. These trumpeting heralds are colored with festive gold spray paint and attached to a pine swag made of cinnamon sticks, citrus fruits, dried seed pods, nuts, berries, and pomanders to create a welcoming seasonal fragrance. Nothing could be simpler.

MATERIALS

¼in/6mm thick medium density fiberboard (MDF) 20 x 32in/50 x 80cm

Jigsaw with medium blade

Gold spray paint

Glue stick

Scissors

Two D rings

Screwdriver

Two ½in/1.5cm slotted brass screws

Garden twine

Masking tape

Fine florists' wire—22 gauge

Fine grade sandpaper

Drill

Two picture hooks and nails

Sprigs of pine boughs, cinnamon sticks, twine, dried flower heads, dried seed pods, dried orange segments, pine cones, acorns, walnuts

1 Make a template by enlarging the pattern provided (p.92) on a photocopier to measure 19in/49cm from the tip of the angel's toe to the end of his trumpet. Draw two on the fiberboard.

2 Cut out two angels. Drill holes in the space between the forearm and chin, large enough to fit the jigsaw blade, then continue cutting. Sand all the edges smooth with fine grade sandpaper. Paint the angels with the gold spray paint, including all the edges. Allow to dry.

3 Find the point of balance and screw a D ring in place with a small brass screw. Take care not to puncture the front of the angel.

4 To make the swag, cut a length of gardening twine to the required length adding enough to your measurement to tie loops at each end. Tie

a long loop at one end and secure the loop to a work surface with a piece of masking tape.

5 Cut pine branches into twigs 6in/15cm long. Cut a small quantity to begin, then more as you need them.

6 Beginning at the secured loop, use wire to tie on the first twig. Hold the next branch in place and wrap the wire around the end of the branch and the twine three times. Wrap the wire back up the branch to stop the materials from sliding. Continue adding pine greenery and tie a long loop in the end.

7 Fill any bare areas by tying in sprigs of pine with short lengths of wire. Decorate the garland by wiring dried fruit, flowers, nuts, and the foliage of your choice into position. Then hang with the gold angels to finish.

house
candle shade

Soften the lighting with these unusual candle holders, inspired by traditional Mexican punched tin light or lantern shades. Made in the form of a simple house, these shades look stunning when the light shines through the windows and the punched holes made by the tracing wheels. The house is illuminated with two votive candles in glass jars for safety, behind translucent tracing paper.

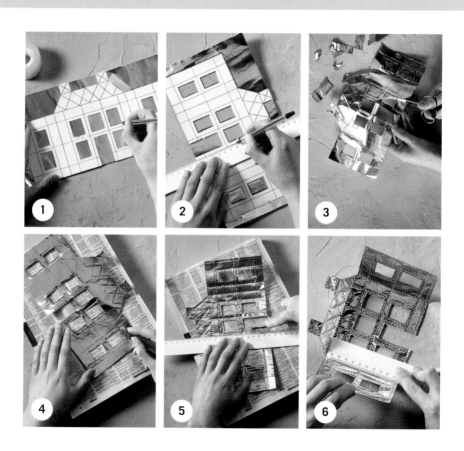

0.004in/0.1mm-thick
aluminum foil
Tracing paper
Glue
Dry ballpoint pen
Ruler and pencil
Craft knife and thin card stock
Two tracing wheels—one with
closely spaced and one with
widely spaced wheels
Old phone book
Small-pointed scissors
Transparent tape

1 Photocopy the pattern provided (p.93) and enlarge to make a template. Stick the photocopy to card stock and cut out. Tape the template to the aluminum foil. Draw the outlines of the house, windows, and door with a dry ballpoint pen, pressing lightly to transfer the shape.

2 Use the ruler and pen to draw lightly over the lines marked on the template—these will appear as indented lines on the metal.

3 Remove the template and carefully cut around it. To cut out the windows, first make a cut in each corner with a craft knife, then push the scissors through.

4 Place the foil right side down on the phone book. Draw lines around the windows with the small tracing wheel, pressing firmly to transfer the design.

5 Using the larger tracing wheel and a ruler, redraw the lightly drawn guide lines. Press very hard so that the points on the wheel pierce through the metal. Use a ruler to draw the straight lines.

6 With the help of a ruler, bend the roof at a 45° angle. Bend the chimneys upright, then bend each side at right angles to the house front.

christmas
wheat sheaf

In rural Scandinavia, wheat sheaves with greenery at their center are traditionally displayed outdoors in front of the home to tempt and sustain birds during the long winter. They are supposed to promise a bountiful Spring. The tradition is founded on the pagan belief that evergreen foliage is the symbol of life renewing itself.

MATERIALS

Approximately 300 stems
of wheat

8–10 stems of holly
with berries

Florists' wire

Small decorative birds

Scissors

Pliers

Garden gloves

Ribbon

1 Wearing gardening gloves, trim each holly stem to 7in/ 18cm long. Trim any leaves from the base of the stems. Make a tightly formed conical shape, then wire the stems together using florists' wire.

2 Holding the holly in one hand, begin applying wheat in small bunches of three or four stems at a time.

Work your way around the holly, holding the wheat stems at an angle. Hold the wheat in place with wire as you work. Continue using the stems until a thick sheaf is formed. Twist wire around the middle of the stems.

3 Trim the bottom of the stems so that they are even. Place the sheaf on a table top and arrange the stems at an angle. With scissors flat to the table surface, trim the stems from the bottom to achieve the desired height. Work from the middle out.

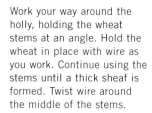

4 Attach 8in/20cm lengths of florists' wire to the small decorative birds. Place each bird in the holly by pushing the wires securely through the holly into the sheaf.

5 Tie the middle of the wheat sheaf with a ribbon in a seasonal color to finish.

paper
gift boxes

Specially wrapped gifts are enticing and appealing and they add to the sense of occasion, so it is worth thinking of interesting and unusual ways to present them. These attractive gift boxes could be filled with tissue paper and used to wrap all kinds of small presents. A simple curl of ribbon on top finishes these simple boxes off and turns them into Christmas tree decorations, as well as gifts.

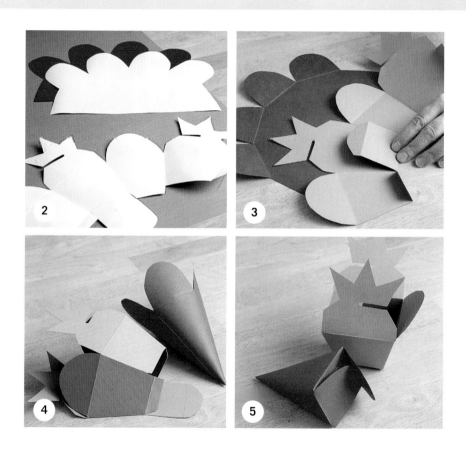

Heavy-weight paper in
your choice of colors

Double-sided transparent tape

Scissors

Paper hole punch

Ribbon or string

Glue stick

1 Enlarge the patterns provided (p.89) and cut out. To make large boxes, enlarge the patterns in sections and stick the pieces together, overlapping and aligning lines as necessary. If you intend to make several gift boxes use cardboard to make the template.

2 Choose your paper for the box. Then, on the wrong side, draw around the template. Mark all fold lines and cut out the outline.

3 For the pineapple box, crease all fold lines. Fold in the sides and secure the side tab on the inside of the box with double-sided tape. Push in the bottom tab and secure as before.

4 Fill the box as desired. Interlink the pineapple top and bend the tab up into a standing position to close.

5 For the cone box, crease all fold lines. Find the center of the long edge for the tip, then overlap the edges of the shape tightly to form a cone. Stick the side edge in place.

6 Hold the cone with the point facing down. Fold each flap flat across the top. Secure the last flap with tape. Make a hole near the tip of the cone using the paper hole punch and thread ribbon or string through it.

chocolate

wreath

This is a modern reworking of the traditional pine wreath and shows just how old ideas can be adapted and updated. A Christmas decoration that can be eaten makes an ideal giftand an enjoyable project for those with a sweet tooth. Colorful foil-covered chocolate insects and bumble bees buzz around orchard fruits with bright butterflies and liqueur-filled orchard fruits.

MATERIALS

Two squares of heavy-weight corrugated cardboard 22in/55cm

Large bundle of pine branches

Foil wrapped chocolates— five or six large and 30 medium or small in assorted designs

Hot glue gun and glue

Florists' wire

Plastic drinking straw

Scissors

Craft knife and cutting mat

Skewer or leather hole punch

Pin and string

1 Draw a 50cm/20in diameter circle on one piece of corrugated cardboard. Tie a pencil to a length of string. Measure 10in/25cm along the string and tie the other end to the pin. Stick the pin in the center of the board. Hold the pencil taut and draw a circle. Center a second circle inside the first, 8in/20cm diameter. Cut out the circles. Discard the center and the outer edges.

2 Place the wreath on the second piece of cardboard with the corrugated lines in opposite directions. Adhere the cut shape to the uncut board using a hot glue gun. Allow to dry. Cut the second piece of cardboard.

3 Make two holes with a skewer 3in/7.5cm from the edge of the cardboard wreath and 3in/7.5cm apart. Push one straw through each hole until the end is flush with

the surface at the back of the board. Glue in place and allow to dry. The straws prevent the hanging wires from tearing the cardboard.

4 Cut one 10in/25cm length of wire and thread through both holes, twist the ends together at the back of the wreath to form a hanging wire.

5 Arrange the largest chocolates in an even pattern on the front of the wreath. Glue the foil in place.

6 Cut long twigs of pine to cover the inside edge of the wreath. Cut shorter twigs to fit between the chocolates. Add twigs to the outside, radiating outwards from the center. Keep the edges neat and cover any bare areas so that the cardboard cannot be seen through the gaps.

7 Glue the remainder of the chocolates onto the pine.

templates

bird greeting card

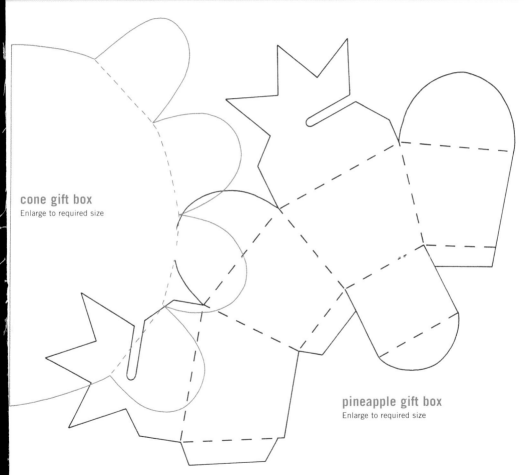

cone gift box
Enlarge to required size

pineapple gift box
Enlarge to required size

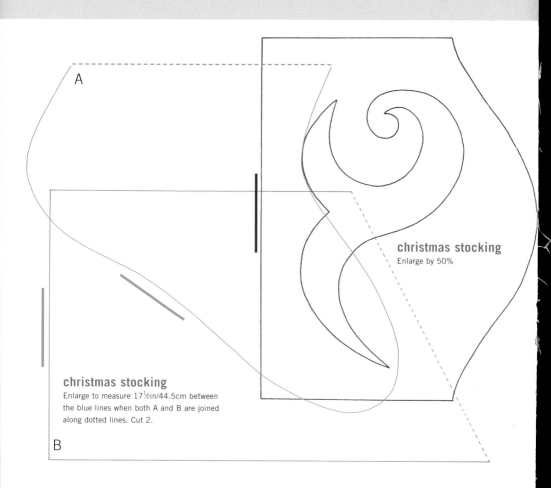

A

christmas stocking
Enlarge by 50%

christmas stocking
Enlarge to measure 17½in/44.5cm between
the blue lines when both A and B are joined
along dotted lines. Cut 2.

B

cut-paper shelf edging
Half the image is shown. Reverse the image at the broken line on the left and increase the depth between the red lines to $5\frac{1}{4}$in/13cm.

felt tree skirt
holly leaf 1

felt tree skirt
holly leaf 2

felt tree skirt
holly leaf 3

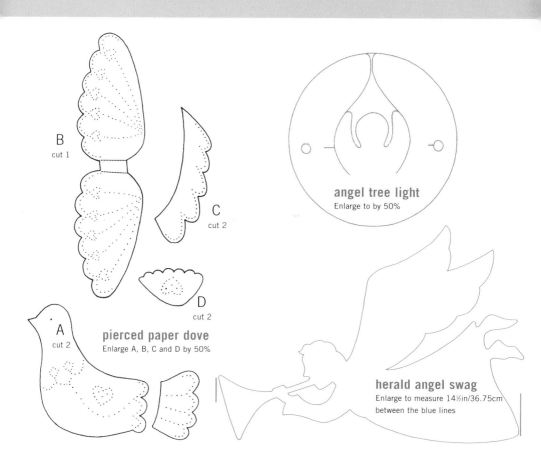

B
cut 1

C
cut 2

D
cut 2

A
cut 2

pierced paper dove
Enlarge A, B, C and D by 50%

angel tree light
Enlarge to by 50%

herald angel swag
Enlarge to measure 14½in/36.75cm
between the blue lines

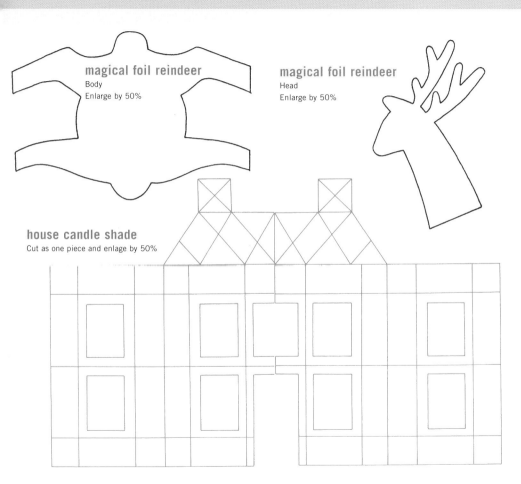

magical foil reindeer
Body
Enlarge by 50%

magical foil reindeer
Head
Enlarge by 50%

house candle shade
Cut as one piece and enlage by 50%

frosted window stencil
Enlarge to fit your window pane

frosted window stencil
Enlarge to fit your window pane

frosted window stencil
Enlarge to fit your window pane